SLIM BLUE UNIVERSE

SLIM BLUE UNIVERSE

BY ELEANOR LERMAN

Mayapple Press 2024

Published by   Mayapple Press
                362 Chestnut Hill Road
                Woodstock, NY 12498
                mayapplepress.com

ISBN 978-1-952781-17-9
Library of Congress Control Number 2023945572

Acknowledgments

These poems originally appeared in the following journals and anthologies:

Tupelo Quarterly/TQ3, The James Dickey Review, The American Journal of Poetry, The Tishman Review, Autumn Sky Poetry Daily, Red Savina, Water-Stone Review, Long Island Quarterly, Nine Mile, Openhearted Poetry Anthology, Valley Voices Literary Review, Trampset, The Sad Girls Club, Crosswinds Poetry Journal, Book of Matches, Bards Annual, Sky Island Journal, Gyroscope Review, The Cumberland River Review, Quiet Diamonds, Nassau County Voices in Verse.

Designed and typeset by Judith Kerman in Constantia with cover title in Calvin. Author photo by Jeff Tiedrich.

CONTENTS

THIEVERY

KARMANN GHIA

Listen,
broken little century
driving around in your Karmann Ghia
like all the rock and rollers,
the queer disciples who
helped me with my homework
in 1968—
I am not done with you.

High as a gilded lily,
slinking around with your bedroom eyes
fixed on Mexico as the
best place to die:

I have the evidence, now,
that you were possessed of
too much hope.
Your clothes were too beautiful;
you were, yourself, too beautiful.
Gay blades indeed: that's a
gut punch, little darling,
little age of pain.

So what were you doing,
drinking the last hours away
in a vicious bar, wearing your
summer suit and a Panama hat?
Setting sail already, hmm?
With your suitcase,
buying a ticket on a passing cloud.

Were you just
waiting to see what would happen?

Well, this is what happened.
At least you could have left me
the keys to the car.

TRUE HEARTS MARRY

When I lived in the city
certain dark yellow hours were
driven straight to my poor, beloved street.
Crates of rain were delivered with the mail.
Old arguments camped out in the kitchen,
old grievances had my number—
but that was how I learned to write.
That was the time when certain deviations
from the norm grew stronger.
I let them. I wanted them to live.

And still, great forces named in schoolbooks
put me to work in the Schoharie Valley,
where the creeks cackled to themselves
as they beat their fists against the houses,
churning out the breakfast biscuits.
People threw pennies at the swans because
that is the currency in normal times:
granite, agate, cold intentions, though perhaps
not in the thoughts of women standing on
the hills above the valley, tall and industrious,
breathing in the chilly blocks of air.

Oh love, how far I have traveled!
Here and there, long and hard.
Heartsick but industrious, I wore
oilskin in the winter, married because
I needed to be married, recovered from
the illnesses that are sold in the stores
of the Schoharie Valley and lied on
the journey that took me halfway
to oblivion. But remember: it is possible
that I also lied on the way back.

So I think that I am old enough now
to have fulfilled my obligations to
the populace. Now I have a new message
for my friends who are gathering in the

poor, impoverished city, where the sun
arises with a new understanding: we thought
we were unhappy, but we were wrong.

So we will get out the old banners,
strip ourselves naked and climb the
battlements of love. Watch the crows
fly towards the city with money in their beaks!
Women are baking the biscuits of resistance,
declaring that they are the brides of time.
Thus am I able to declare that I have loved
my work with bread that is stronger than
any winter in a northern valley. *I love, I am,*
I do what I can to resist the deliveries of death
and poverty. I speak to women in my sleep.

But remember: women never sleep
when they are in the city. True hearts
marry upon the battlements and only age
in the fleeting thoughts of swans.

THE RAG-AND-BONE GOOD-BYE

Listen, I remember what you wore
those hot nights in the city: the rags,
the satin, and then the slim blue universe
that opened for you at two a.m.
No one worked in those days. Doors opened,
assignations poured out like water from
a river bronzed and gleaming with love.

Or not love: more likely, pain. Everyone
was too young then; everyone was queer
and reveled in it. Doors opened and we
walked through; we did anything that
was suggested. Well, perhaps not me:
I think I was making an assessment.
I think I did not have the right clothes.
I think I ached more than I wanted
anything—and yet, I wrote down everything
you said to me every time you walked away.

So here it is, my rag-and-bone good-bye:
the moon will be dust, the days
will be dust, the nights will cough up a silver
river of stars and I will still be writing
all this down. I know what your argument
would be: that I refused to speak for
years and years—and that is true,
but I am speaking now, each word
a slim blue universe, each line an
opening door. Come home at last,

wearing your silver shoes. Footsteps
can break the glass silence; each day
comes closer to the end, each night
is built again when you appear.

A WAVE CAN BE A PARTICLE

Here is the problem: that the life the body
contains may not be the same as the life
that the mind imagines. Indeed, the suspicion grows
as time expands that we are hiding things
from ourselves. Big things, shaped like nebulae
or chandeliers; in other forms, they express velocity.
They are going so fast that we doubt we saw them,
but we did. Before and after we were born, we did.

We do. Which is why the suspicion grows
that laid out on a cold bed in the dying light
may only be the fate of bones. That there is, perhaps,
another example to consider: as a wave can be
a particle and a particle a wave, you need not
chain yourself to the belief that a steady state
is the singularity that holds all value

but may think, instead, of the feeling
that comes over you in the moment before
a weeping ghost appears to you (and only you?)
from the darkness beyond the bedroom door,
or when you approach the threshold that
must be crossed as you go into the woods
and find yourself upon the hidden path that,

rumor has it, leads directly into the void,
but step, instead, into another springtime.
On the flowering lawn, a girl you swear
that you once knew is laughing, and
all around her (but not only her),
the windy sky is full of stars.

THIEVES

She sits in a window seat on a rainy afternoon and thinks
      about the thieves.
Last seen, one was under the influence in London,
another was getting a haircut in Paris. The dark one
was boarding a plane to Ibiza, the most brilliant was still
      living in Hydra,
or so they say. One death is recorded: the thief who
      ran away to Goa.
India, India: he rode a bus to Nepal to buy an American passport
but turned around and came back. India had bought his heart
with its dusty sunsets, its routes east, where he could trade for
      all the old drugs.

These were her teachers. Whatever they stole was what she learned
to love. And what is left? A jewel in a dresser drawer, a dress in an
      empty closet
and memories of American discotheques, which create routes
      of their own,
winding through the rain towards nights she wore like jewelry.
Dancing, dancing: boyfriends were easy to get in those days.
She could steal their hearts and they would tell her things,
      give her even more.
But this is what she is learning now: that time
      abhors us all.
I did not say that it ignores us, which may be what
      you expected:
this is her story, not mine, not yours, and this
is what she believes: that time has already
eaten all the angels. They tasted like cake, but they
      are all gone.

And of course, there is no window seat: she invented that
because she saw it in a movie: a pretty girl, too young
      to remember anything,
remembers what she can. Around here, the gray weather
      reinvents itself every morning

though it has no skill, no new ideas: it wears clouds
instead of a bandana, and the clouds only slouch
        through the sky.
They are fearful. It is a fearful time.

But soon, she will raise her hand in magic
because yes, she can still do this. And she will name
the name of every thief who, in life and death, will
        still hear her.
In life and death: that is what she believes.

Don't you?

SAFE PASSAGE

In this house, now, where twilight has become
my name, there is only one hour left, or perhaps
more—who can tell? If nothing happens, then I
will go to sleep. Birds tell me what to dream,
or ghosts do, or the prophesying moon.

In the morning, I am walking the roads
carrying a sack, going nowhere. I feel
that I have been sentenced to wander
in the western lands, but what does that
even mean? My name is nothing any more.
Twilight overspreads me and I walk on,
I walk on. Ghosts try to feed me.
The moon sizzles. There are no birds.

And every house I enter now, I must leave.
I can feel it: the summing up, the letting go,
the last time for everything, which no one
has ever shared. There are creatures in the
twilight that know my name: I will ask them
for safe passage and I believe that they will
grant it as a good deed, pleasing to God—

or so I have been told.

TABLES AND CHAIRS

I know what I look like
in the supermarket buying
jam and bread instead of
cooking up a plan, or

tidying up behind the bank,
hoping for an accidental delivery
while I carry my little dog around
in a shoulder holster—

old and foolish. Not dangerous
anymore, plus unemployed: just a
kid without a kingdom, a babushka
smacked around by the wind.

Ha! She thinks that little dog can shoot.
And she still believes that she was born
in a monsoon season, in a bloody year.
But who cares except the hospital?

Who cares? Perhaps the tables
and chairs that open up the
morning café and let me pay with
coins that represent sincerity

because if I can carry all that remains
in a single pocket then life will go on
for a few more hours. Then messages
will arrive in envelopes of pain

that taste like orange marmalade.
That was the plan all along, devised
in the playland of loss, dementia
and ruin: to eat what was served

and say nothing about it. To tell
my secrets to no one but the little dog,
who represents eternity. To wear
the wind like a scarf and let the body

stand out in the rain, if that's what it wants,
if that will ease its suffering, poor thing.
As if suffering exists. As if the fortune tellers
hired by the state are right in their prediction
that only one more bloody year

will pass until the infinite comes crashing
through the skylight and dinner cooks itself.
As for me, I am waiting to be saved by anyone
who loves their pet. Or a girl on a bicycle,

a boy in a dream. I am dreaming
of the way out of my dilemma: to live
because I want to or because it is really
jade that represents sincerity,

pale green jade and white flowers
that remain after the fires go out,
after I use the embers to make a necklace
that I will wear when I go shopping with

the little dog, who represents the time
that I have left. Which I will use as
best I can. Which is what I am doing now,
trying to help the broken heart of tomorrow

to buy its medication. Which is how I spend
whatever I can earn: one penny at a time,
one dog day after another, one little life,
one beating heart. Which is what I believe:

that only thus may we embrace
again in the shopping malls of time,
in the lanes and alleys where we were
really born. So read this as a signal that
all is forgiven. That the tables and chairs

are cooking up a plan that will cost us
nothing. That will let us walk out into the
dusty morning and partake, like good citizens
and blessed hooligans, of all that remains.

RADIOS

This is a lonely epoch.
Before, there was so much time spent
in hotels, so much cold marble to
sleep on. Drinks and drugs and dark meals
no one remembers. We disowned the genders,
dressed them as we wished while we watched
from burning tables in the clubs,
from broken windows on the highest,
cheapest floors. The city lived its life

and we lived ours: lost streets, lost years,
lost days and nights when we called each other
to make arrangements, to spend each other's
money in dangerous ways. Oh, I loved
everything then. Does it sound like I didn't?
Does it sound like it may have been too much?
It never was. I could have taken more.

But this is a lonely epoch, now.
I assign no blame for all the mild love
that has come to haunt the city,
the empty metropolis. Asleep on a couch,
with a book in my hand and medicine
in my blood, I still dream about
the city. (Behold its junkie's heart,
its messages scratched out in graffiti!)
I still dream about the city
as we all do. As we should,

because in the new epoch, there is
a radio in every room of my house.
All of them speak to me with old voices
and what I hear is: *Let my stories be true,*
let what I remember belong to me,
let a flower fall from a vase on the porch
on this one summer afternoon.

Because any moment now,
any moment

THE SISTERS OF TOMORROW

If they come again,
the mad and angry years
when the sisters of tomorrow
run through the streets in dirty
nightgowns, chased by the police,
just tell them I am poor again,

and once again bereft.
My jewelry is gone
and all my intimate letters.
They held the memories in which
I met with beautiful boys in
music shops. Music was always
playing. We corresponded by airmail.
We believed in true romance.

So I wish that I had more to say
but a thousand times I've tried
to explain and a thousand times
I've failed. If more time was allotted
to speak again, I would say that
I was imprisoned because I lived
alone too long. And I would apologize

for growing older when all I meant
to do was put on a beautiful hat.
But I couldn't change, I couldn't stop:
I valued my work above all else
And this is my work: you have it
in your hands.

Now, a thousand years go by,
a thousand times I run away.
But I run towards nothing; the
bejeweled ambassadors of
sorrow are already here, sewing
more nightgowns. Calling the police.

But you say, *Don't be afraid:*
a wooden boat laden with oranges
is already sailing home across
blue waters. A little book of love
sits on a table in a quiet house.

A thousand years go by,
a thousand times I run away.
But you say, *Come back, little darling*
Everything is bound to get better—
and despite the stony silence
of tomorrow, it does.

REMINISCENCE

I am still alive tonight. Sleepless, yes, but
still alive. And Richard Brautigan's lightbulb
is still burning. One of us will have to put it
out soon—better us than them. And once
the house has gone dark, let's find a brute
of a dog to place at the head of the column
as we march away. If we've learned anything,
surely it is that at times like these, it pays
to leave some beloved antiquity untamed.

Later, if you want to reminisce, I suggest
you do it while you're still strong enough
to see that it's all there, the whole story:
in the summer night, in the upstairs
bedroom with the open window,
in the dream you had of a quiet city
where you believe that we once lived,

in the joy expressed by small kisses, in
the color of chrysanthemums, of afternoons
spent in cafes, in what we wrote
on walls. In what we took with us.
And how we run to embrace even
the last ones out despite knowing, now,
what we would always have to leave behind.

NITROGLYCERIN

The morning is a clock. The evening is a painful puzzle.
What, I wonder as I wander through the house,
is still holding the world upright upon its ancient
alabaster pillars? Rage, perhaps, that cocky old bird
with its black wings and gimlet eye. Or grief, which
wanders with me in a ragged nightgown eating slices
of nitroglycerin cake. All I can say is well, yes,

these were our lives, constructed inside a cage of fate.
Inside a crazy house, inside a burning ball rolling down
a burning hill. Sweeping through the foreign cities,
monsters in gorgeous dresses dressed up and danced
while the wind swept through their heart of hearts,
my heart, your heart, until nothing mattered anymore.

Or that is the message the news brings: that nothing
matters anymore. But if that is true, why did I bother
to escape from the infirmary? Sick as the milk
in the broken hotel, old as the years of sleeping in,
I watch the sun crack and shower sparks upon my plate.

But here is the news inside a lotus blossom, inside
the color of the scarf you wore when we were young:
I am running now. The clocks are running in the hotels.
The cities are running all over the world, tripping
on the chain mail they made women wear in
medieval movies. We can work this out if you
promise to be good. I will be bad enough for
both of us, live long enough to nail this note
upon the brainless face of the dead-end sun.

And tomorrow, we will place the children in
a basket of bulrushes and go knock down palaces
and pyramids. No one shall be born a slave
in my house and the new beasts will adore us
because cleverly, we have set the old ones free.

To Live in This World Requires

To live in this world requires
that you leave your house every morning
and step into the wind.
Every morning: with all your memories
on file and the future pinned to some wall
you will have to build and tear down and
build again. If you get there. If. If.

Into the wind: first you walk the dog whose
blessed face belies the beast that it is built upon.
Millennia behind you, that beast enters a cave
and decides whether or not to kill a child sleeping
by a fire. It does not kill the child
because its heart has been surprised by love:
both softened and sharpened by it, inexplicably.
Inexplicably, to this day.

And on this day, the wind relents.
The morning star lifts itself into a changeable sky
and you, carrying extra weight, wearing
last year's clothes, start walking towards the train.
Seeds that grew from ancient science digest
in your stomach; your bones begin to separate
because science did not plan this length of life.
Your heart slows down and you feel
the pressure of dragging a million, billion years
behind you. A million, billion lie ahead
that you will know nothing about.

Thus, harnessed to time, facing the inevitable,
constructed by science and fed on inexplicable events
taking place somewhere in the middle of history,
your day goes by. Miles away, the ocean
murmurs to its own beloved creatures, a mountain
applies pressure to the weaving of a golden seam.
And in your house, the dog wonders if you
will make it home again. And each day, despite
or because the performance of this feat is both
a mystery and a triumph, somehow you will.
You do.

THE BOOK OF DEVOTION

My time is short.
I have to find a way to express
my argument against the commanders:
I thought that if I survived the rainy streets
and low spirits, the fake prints of Paris
rotting in the dark would be enough to
get me out of this, to recommend me

to the goodwill of the angels
but apparently I was mistaken.
My heart staged a rebellion but
nothing has been decided except
that I should fight on, alone.

So never mind. When I was sick,
I dreamed that my mother's arms
enfolded me. I visited a golden museum
where dead statues offered me a choice
and I came back because I wanted to.

Harken to the loss: she spoke
and I listened, but I lost the art of
hearing so I had to crawl. I bought
blouses that didn't fit, lived in
apartments with cats that prowled
the empty spaces between the walls

and I tried, I tried. Do you hear me?
I am trying still. I travel on windy
days, I visit doctors, I behave. I am
trying to age as best I can. I take my
medicine as prescribed, sit on the porch

and speak pleasantly to passersby.
Flowers bloom in the vases that I
buy with my own money. No one
would ever guess that I once
owned a vampire suit. That I
caught one of those cats and kept it.

Well, what did you think?
That I wouldn't still want
to turn my own pages?
Indelible heart, rise up and defend me!
I know there is a book of devotion.
I know there is a radiant way.

LONG DAYS ALREADY GREENING

If, on a ruined day, there is
lonely music playing in an empty room
and the sun, in dull ashen sadness, sweeps
itself off the stage, and the moon goes mad,
and your arms are full of birds—

then think that this is how I have always loved you.
Traveling, traveling, we missed each other
by years and years, but what does that matter?
I am still yours.

In this late hour, with one lamp lit
and time wandering in the kitchen
looking for what is left that it might eat,
I still want to believe that we were
born for this:

To deceive the dead and fool the living
just long enough to make it to the
endless road that we have walked before
and will walk again. For this is how
I have always loved you: here and there,
a soul, a being, bright and burning, dangerous
up to the last minute because I believed
that I could change my life.

You are my witness. But be careful:
we cannot know what long days
already greening in some ancient pasture
still think that we are slaves.

TALES OF THE HIGH DESERT

I was in a car on a lost road
traveling through the high desert.
I was not driving so I had time to think
and what I came up with was,
Jews don't stand a chance out here.
Then I remembered how all this started:
same people, different desert,
that spectacular crisis of faith.

I began to believe that the car
had magic headlights.
The constellations swam through the sky.
They flapped their wings and told me stories
about The Little Ice Age, which followed
The Medieval Warming Period,
and of course I believed them when
they issued a statement about how
they remembered all of that
and a whole lot more.

In the next town, I asked the car
to stop and it liked me, so it did.
I went into a store and bought
a quart of milk and a healing stone
but later, when I went to make
a meal out of differential objects
all I could find in the bag was
a little dog. Lucky for me,
it liked me, so it stayed alive.

But in the here and now,
in this ordinary house
with only ordinary books to read,
I have no choice but to behave.
Sometimes a car pulls up (one of
the mean ones) and makes a
mockery of everything I've

ever written. It demands payment
and it is the little dog who
volunteers to go to work.

And so I weep because I have no choice now
but to pretend I am a nice girl.
I weep because the desert is alone.
I weep because time is a weight
that the little dog has always carried in
a little purse and I have always known it,

yet love drives me on. The little dog
whispers directions and swears to me
that it is still hoping for the best.

INEVITABLE

It was years ago that you came home.
Years ago that I took you back into my arms.
The cloudy winter wrapped itself around
my thoughts as they piled up in the
in the front room like a pile of old stoves.
You fooled the ambassador in Khartoum
who mistook opium for soap and
sent you off on an airplane, looking
like a young king soaked in blood.

So why did you come home to me,
bringing boxes of immortal dirt reminiscent
of the past? I needed money, I needed
a spell that I could count on, I needed
a doctor, and protection from the future.

Did you think of that at the crossroads,
or when the dusty trails that stretched
from dawn to dusk began to wave
good-bye, good-bye? I always wanted
to write this down while I was young,
while I had talent, and in the time
when nothing hurt as badly
as everything hurts now.

The luster of chalcedony will not
heal me, nor Buddha's speculations.
Cats have no power anymore,
not that I can see. And the future
is tapping its foot. Inevitably, it awaits.

So good-bye, good-bye.
The parts of my body that are still hospitalized
will always remember you.
Time is baking on the stove and I am wheeled
from room to room, looking for one more box.
It is inevitable that I will find it.
Inevitable that I will look inside.

SOMEONE NEW

All through the spring evening, there is
the longing for Jerusalem. Dates and figs,
        water and wine.
If these were not my own memories, I would
        renounce them
but I know that they are real. Breathless afternoons,
hot and gold and dusty. That is what one longs for,
really, having emigrated to the new world, having
expected what is as old as time—promises, of course,
and what always follows: ruin. Intrigue. Rot and rebirth.

Then a letter arrives from Paris. It speaks of the
women and girls who have gone there for the shopping.
Soon, they will fly away home, clasped in the embrace
of their beautiful dresses woven out of prayers.
Prayers for the lost Jew, for the lonely Christian
        and for their holy longing.
We were with them once, we were all there,
in the beginning, before all this, all that

Sitting at my mother's table is a recollection
that still belongs to me. She kisses me and all
        the stars fall from the sky.
Memory, memory: say it is not too late to
gather together in someone's name and then
        name him.
Name someone walking home, someone
who knows nothing yet. Someone coming
        in the dusty, golden spring
Someone our broken hearts cannot
remember. Oh yes, please: someone new.

Observe the Age of Comings and Goings

Where are you traveling? Supposedly, wherever
your ticket says, though all you can remember
of your movements in years gone by is that
there was some vague appointment to be kept
in a distant city. Perhaps, if it was a sunny day,
there was a place where you would have stopped
to eat lunch.

But where are you going now? There was a plan,
once, to seek out Ilion—do you remember?
To ingest whatever was being sold in the markets
and slap the faces of those flat-faced, marble beauties,
the ancients who would not answer us. Who conceived
their revenge in the shape of beasts and whirlpools.
Who pretended that they knew things that we
did not.

So why are you packing? Who told you
that you have to go? Instead, you should ask
who enslaved you, who tied you to the years
and broke them like rocks into hours and
days and abandoned them on your doorstep.
Who made these rules? Who threw stars at you
but lied about their power to beat inside you
like a heart?

Remember the promise of resistance.
Remember that for every train that leaves
the station, the power of the observer diminishes
as he or she (your choice) watches it depart.
Besides, he—or she—will soon forget you,
just in time to ply their trade with others who
are more—well, let's say, *desirable.* Expect that:
your only job now is to loosen your grip on the
observer. Observe: the age of comings and goings
is almost past.

All that is left is to fight your way into
the great hall of invisible forces and tear up
the timetables. *Time tables.* Then the marble hands
will pretend to applaud you and all the seasons
will send you messages from the future,
which you are entitled to read where and when
you want to. *If* you want. If you haven't already
acquired a war dog and a generation of allies
whose ruthless dreams are finally scheduled
to come true.

NINE AT THE BEGINNING

This is what I see tonight:
you sitting on a mattress
in that old building on St. Marks
with your Greek hair and suggestive hands
casting pennies with the Book of Changes—
love had its own strategies, then,
love with its grocery store lilies
more fragrant than fate.

But fate fell all around us then
like snow. Winter carried soup
and candles down the hallway
of the old building on St. Marks.
We were too young to be cold, too sure
we couldn't be saved to care that knowledge
was a burden we would carry with us always.
In fact, that was what we expected:
vampires for lunch and dinner.
Vampire lovers, vampire life.

This is what I see tonight:
you showing me the coins that say
Nine at the beginning means waiting
in the meadow. It furthers one to abide
in what endures. Which is why I am giving you
all that I can while I am still armed with your
unexpected love: here is a harpsichord,
a book of marriages, my one good shirt.
My picture of the vampires
holding hands at the grocery store.
They didn't know what to buy for you.
They never will.

Poor things, with their renegade hearts
and failed predictions: it's a hard winter
we have to walk these days with our
hard steps banging on the eternal stairs—
Darling, I have never burned your letters
I am living in the city now and write

books about you that always begin
with winter coming down hard upon
an unexpected meadow.

There are crimes
that were committed in the past
but the future forgives them—
You walk through the door
and I can stop crying
even though the night is endless
and will be full of lies.

DOLL FACE

Back when I had a doll face and
a Russian laugh that could punch a mountain
in the teeth, I knew how to shop in the underworld,
in the night stores where dust and wind dressed
as perfectly as dark angels and bought
lovely lies for their mysterious companions.
Back when foreigners slept in exotic beds
and all was well.

But then they—*whoever they are*—
published the instructions to watch
as modern love progressed. I wouldn't
do it, though: instead I watched the skies
and detected sinister intentions that I
approved of. What can I say? I always
knew the difference between an assault
on reason and observing women
gazing at the moon.

But what shall I do now that I have been
diagnosed with the need to rent a room
at the brazen seaside that will shamelessly
outlive me? My last convalescence made me
furious; this one won't stop thinking
about itself.

So in my letter to the editor of this
ridiculous publication, I will enclose
an untimely cat and a sinister hello.
That's what I think, as time marches on
in its high heels and laughing jackboots:
someone once cheated someone, but listen,
babycakes and cutie pies: *Ha ha!*
It won't be me.

My Dears and Darlings

Lightning kept me up last night.
It kept us all up, I suppose
in this electric world of overloaded
wires, where we sizzle in our beds,
where "Death Stalks the Infinite"
is the only program ever made.
No commercials, only innuendo.
It plays on and on, on everyone's tv.

So my dears and darlings,
where to next? It would be
a pleasure to zoom around
the universe in a close embrace
but you're dressed wrong and I
am drunk. (At least, I hope
I am.) Besides, I haven't slept
in a thousand years. Have you?

Beneath the sea there are behemoths
who would befriend us if we were not
so nearly out of time, good looks,
good drugs. Behemoths who would
share their homes with us and co-sign
for our debts. We could float up
to the surface if we wanted.
Nothing would ever hurt.

Instead, bad dreams crack open
with electric woe. Gut-sick women
address the multitudes and time,
time, time, piles on the pain.
Hear the crowds roar, the
wrong guesses defile the
best guesses we ever made.

And my guess? My last remark?
That at least one particle of life will
refuse to suffer. It will zoom around

the universe with zest and verve and
all of that, and with a clear conscience,
take a nap in front of the tv.

It has a cause, a credo, and a house
inching ever closer to a sea of friends.
It is actually watching for the lightning.
It is listening to women's warnings.
It has a multitude of sinful sisters,
not one of them afraid.

The Younger Self

The younger self is drinking in a bar
off Washington Square. Is it too young, really,
to be served? That doesn't matter since it
no longer inhabits its physical form.
It only exists, now, at the tail end of
a ghost generation that has scattered
not to the winds, exactly, but to
houses in the mountains, houses
at the shore, where clouds come in
through the windows, thinking that
they hear familiar music. Perhaps they do.
Some of us remember. Some do not.

The younger self would like you—
yes, *you*—to get on a train, come back,
come home, come live that life again.
It is difficult not to try because something
might still be there: the cold room on the
side street in the beloved city; soup in the pot,
the red jar that held the better medicine,
and the stars that came in through
the windows. In those days, they knew
how to speak, which is amusing, now,
since all the stories they told us were lies.

The younger self calls on the phone
every morning. Clouds in its brain,
stars on the plate instead of breakfast
and still, it is beautiful. It is a beautiful girl
who can drink away the day, who dresses
like an actress, who does not care that the dog
worries it would be left alone or that the work
you do now is harder. Much harder.
But you have to do it. You want to do it.
You begin it every hour, again and again.

The younger self, perhaps, is growing
impatient with us. It thinks that it
might just want us to pass this note along

to others who will undoubtedly know
how to reach her. So here it is.
Don't even tell her that we said hello.

VOICES FROM BEYOND

GHOSTS ARE WATCHING ME

These are shell days.
Echoes in the ear have names
and what they name is on a list
          of things you wanted.
What *did* you want in those
unremarkable times when
what was in your pocket
          could buy the world?

Now, every little thing that
          was wasted
walks down the street in the
early morning and waits for you
at the bus stop, wanting to
          hold your hand.
Of course there is weeping.
Years later, the letters that
          came in the mail
told us this was what
          should be expected.

And now, in my house,
ghosts are watching me.
My plan is to uninvite them
          because I am not finished.
I never bought anything that
I couldn't put a spell on
          and I still feel dangerous.
Sometimes, anyway.

So look outside:
night falls and the creepy crawlies
prowl the street, their bodies
          made of stars.
That's what *I* expected
Sometimes, in the company of
such gorgeous maniacs
          all I can do is laugh.

Modern Intentions

If I were not so lonely
I would tell you about the days
gone by, and I would
remember them as I choose.
So: the beloved little house,
the flowers blooming in
the sunny doorway,
the little dog upon a cushion.

Alternatively, great clocks bellow.
Wars begin. I am sick again
in a house of sickness and
I never marry. I forget my name.

Or you could walk with me
under the wingspan of a bird
in the rain, a memory bird
getting its bearings,
dripping lotus water, wary,
but eternally unharmed.

Walk with me. If I were not so
lonely, I would admit that all
I am afraid of lies backwards
and forwards across the head
of a pin. Meaning, I doubt
that I am made of starlight.

Though when I was a child,
I could lie in bed and watch
mysterious trains approaching
from the great beyond.
They were bending towards me
bearing pieces of the night.

Oh pins and blossoms,
trains and clocks and war!
Oh great night beyond

my ability to write this down
in the language of love—

I thought my passage to
the morning would be
open to interpretation,
like a charm upon a bracelet
given with modern intentions
to a girl who lived
a long time ago.

Rehoboth

for R.L.H.

In this county of sand and sea air
we are good companions: patient, rich
for a day. We can buy anything we want
though I want nothing—it is enough
to walk behind you carrying the bags
of dresses, shoes, necklaces and rings.
This is the Village of Sighs, where
cool hands touch each object: the
salesgirls all have perfect lovers who
make them happy, so they always know
the right item to offer when you walk
into their shop. And they know
a beautiful girl when they see one:
what can they do but wait while you
walk between the bolts of silk:
ice blue, ice green, yellow for magnolia.
Beautiful girl on a beautiful day in
a seaside town. I am grateful;
I always will be. Now, the evening
gathers like smoke in the foothills.
How much I love you. How much more
I was always willing to spend.

LATE JULY

What we are forced to deal with now
is the heart of the matter,
which has only been revealed after
a slew of complaints. So picture this:

what is essential to the government
is likely just a rumor to the rest of us.
Besides, it is already late July
and we have not received our dinner.
We have not been allowed to
go outside to play.

Under such conditions, who can say
what next will walk through the door
of some local establishment and make
an attempt to convince humanity

that the body's desire
to lay itself upon the far horizon
is a reasoned stance and not simple sadness?
Still, it may be time to admit
that the body has been a friend
to all, but in the end,

not a true companion: too many nights
it howled alone in its rotting bed.
So let it go where it will go,
wearing a locket that holds
a picture no one can identify.

What can that matter now?
Already, it is late July.
The household gods are
abandoning the household.
They run through the golden fields,
stabbing at the sun with
salad forks and butter knives.

If I had a home to go to I would burn
it down myself and take up arms
for a good cause—if I could think
of one at this late stage of life

because now I know why
love stops at roadside inns
to weep in the arms of strangers—

Only travelers can say when day is done
and they have taken to the roads of
hither and yon, stopping to weep

in the arms of women
whose few small gestures are the
priceless remnants of our dreams of joy.

BIBLE FOOD

This is the morning: small breaths and stumbles.
Not a knife fight in sight. Not a floorboard that
isn't ready to rise up and barricade the room.
The ringing in my ears is the waste of love:
        kites, green fields, spring breezes.
Who can really remember these things?
Now leave me alone: I have to go douse myself
in what is left of the household's supply of flames.

But inevitably, I am back. Half a fish for lunch,
half for dinner: this is bible food all right, as if
that could fool the angels banging at the door.
They are not pious or even polite—that kind
        was of a different generation:
ours come with broken bones and nerve damage,
and they bite. Would you like to see my scars?
They're not nearly as attractive as they used to be.

Half a fish for lunch, half for dinner.
What verse are we on now? One beyond
the last page of any sacred scripture, I presume,
judging by the infinite emptiness outside
        the window,
by the little dogs—the only good souls in
this story—coming back to guide me because
I'm going blind to "the way things used to be."

The evidence? I lose washcloths and
shoes and medicines as easily as I will
lose this poem now that you have read it.
Once a proud assassin, these days I am
        humbled and hungry
or so I appear. We appear. Those of us
pretending to be sweet as pie because
we need your help to spread the message
But don't look for us. Perhaps there is
no message. Your guess is as good as mine.

HASHISH

The evening air is gold, a gold curtain,
an eastern dream as the blonde is just
getting out of bed. It is her heart that we saw
in all the paintings that hung in all the studios
on Renwick Street in 1969. So let's leave her there
for now: she still needs to get cigarettes.
And she still believes that she has another decade
of nights in the cafes and coffee shops.
Perhaps she does.

And perhaps the trade routes are still open,
though the years have taken their toll: I can't
eat, I can't sleep, I can't keep going back and
forth as if I wasn't there—yes, still, *there*—
and yet get out of bed roiling in the here and now.
In the here and now, hashish would kill me;
music does. In the cafes and coffee shops,
I'd have no chance.

Peace, I thought. At least I will have peace.
But in this time of all times, it is rumored
that April will never come again: the quiet rain,
the rainy afternoon, the sun arising, afterwards,
to send us walking in the park...This is not what
I want, to look off in another direction but
now, supposedly, it is required. By whom?
And why? Well, who can say?

I say these free days may begin with coffee
and end with gin, but please, take care
when you slip back into my life.
Take care of me carelessly, as if no one
had ever broken my painted heart.

Princess X

Where have you gone,
my button-faced bride
with your love spooling out
into the universal neighborhood?

First you put ideas into my head
and then refuse to let me
arrange them into a bouquet.
I think I would feel better
if I had to do less sewing

and had more energy to devote
to helping my typewriter
finally complete its reflections
on the meaning of life
if there even is a good one
left on the shelf.

Come on, give a kid a break—
as time goes on, I am becoming
more and more afraid of the dark.
More links are stolen from my
daisy chain and believe me,
I am down to just a few,

which is why the gang and I
(what's left of them, of me)
are so confused about why
we're still working such
long hours when the payoff
in rhyme and reason is hardly
enough to keep a soliloquy alive.

And yet, here comes the parade
that will elect you to the position
of Princess X, both a scandal and
a cutie, too busy to be admired

but admired—wildly!—nonetheless.
Even when the lights go out,
even when there is nothing
that can be fixed, you will be

driving cars around dangerous bends
with your finest, fiercest hairdo
perfectly in place. And I suppose
that I will still be home with the children

fearing the worst. Look, if I bake a pie
in your honor, will you let me go?
How I wish that art for art's sake
would stand up for itself. Or at least,
give me an address that I can write to

in order to demand a refund. After all,
that there's nothing less professional
than a once-a-week blue moon.

WHEN WOMEN PINNED THEIR THOUGHTS UPON THE BREEZES

In a time of soft suede gloves
that bought themselves for women's
hands and department stores were
on the main line, on the telephone,
beautiful bracelets were arrayed
in splendor, like love everlasting

and it was easier to admit the morning
into my life. With sand and gold,
in that time of life, we built a little
courtyard between our houses
where we could sit with our thoughts
about the weather gleaming
and glittering in the breeze,

while art was in the workroom, hammering
itself into my name. *Art,* I whispered
as I laid my head beneath the saw, glad to be
cut into pieces, into poems. Into the
ribbons and wires and cherry blossoms
that built the harpsichords on those mornings
when you were in the garden and I
was still crossing the courtyard of my life.

Art makes me whole, but only sometimes,
only when it contains the memory of you
that I could not revisit until I found
the language in which you spoke to me
in the days of harpsichords and bracelets,
when women pinned their thoughts
upon the breezes and let them fly away.

So take your time in dressing for the day.
Search high and low for your beautiful gloves:
no one will die while they are reading this

and the morning will arise in artful splendor.
All you did for me is written in the language
that was hidden in my back pocket—
I have it now. Now the real work can begin.

Friends of the Filmmaker

Are you afraid
because a gun arrived
in a box of apples? I think
that belongs outside our neighbors'
door, the people who still believe
that it is possible to beg or barter
for something sweet.

But in this life, now, pain and trouble
have no need to make subtle advances.
I think they like to swagger
down the street and break
a few windows. I think

they are the kind of guys
who won't take no for an answer.
They don't write letters anymore.
They don't disguise their voices
on the phone.

So don't pray outside the hospital:
the beds can't hear you.
The medicines prescribed in the
throes of bad dreams
have problems of their own—

They are bewitched;
they are the victims of grievous errors;
they are locked up in a museum of
useless curatives. It is too late for them,
for that, for anything at all.

Or maybe not.
What if I build you a clavichord
that will clear its gentle throat
with the utmost love and longing?
What if I buy you a dress
with baroque intentions

and take you to a shop on
St. Mark's Place where a
dying magician will sell you
the rights to his documentary

in which we both appear as
Friends of the Filmmaker
as if we were going to be together
always,

as if, when the great bells ring
in the land of wolves, flowers
will set the clocks back to another time
and when you come into my arms

none of this will ever happen
and fruit will ripen in the very moment
that you hold it in your hand.

A Walk in the Spring with My Dog

Well yes, it takes medicine now and will, plus
the kind of footgear that a wild child
just down from the barricades would expect
to anchor the costume of an elder:
an old party, new to the game

which apparently begins now: as others
gather to march, we are stepping off
into the winds of tomorrow. The trees
part like a gate for The Dog Who Believes
That She Will Live Forever. Green grass,
yellow flowers, silver-running creeks:
all that, again and again, year after year.
Why should it be otherwise?

Why? Because the winds have invaded
my house, so there is no turning back.
The cups and saucers have been put away.
The bed has fallen through the floor.
Now, only the dreams of the dog know how
to clean the rooms. Only the dreams of
the dog filter down through the sunlight

and reveal the way. Now is the time of
lonely steps: human time, but with
an animal's seeing eye. Thus, the
days arrive like letters in the wind

and open themselves fearlessly
while we wait to breathe.

MY METAPHORS

Somewhere in the neighborhood of lies
I boarded a bus and came straight here.
Or should I say, that's what it feels like
though I remember the music and the
quilts that comforted me in the

East Village days. Sick or stoned, I went
to work and pounded out my metaphors:
lilacs and marzipan for lunch,
eyes hunched in my pocket,
secretly observing the glittering days.
Don't you remember? Don't you agree?

Honey of my heart, these are the
other days, the leftovers. The ones that
hurt and defile. I used to lay out
my clothes are if a shirt could wrap me
in magic. As if time wanted to live the way
that I lived. As if it wished me well.

But now that I am here and all
transportation has been suspended
I ache and stumble and churn the days
into summer clouds to be hung up
on the line. If that's all that they
are good for now, then I can't sleep
in this bed anymore. I can't pretend
that my thoughts are not, now,
thinking for themselves.

So I will set out on my own,
with my name sewn inside my clothes
and boots I stole from a storybook.
I will be traveling across the windy landscape,
I will skirt the edge of reason with my
brain in my backpack, my ability
to speak cut into shreds.

Don't come after me. Don't try to give me money.
My body is already shopping for another life
because, like any old friend, it still thinks
it can meet me at the border and, disguised
as a bird of paradise, follow me across.

VISITING THE RUINS

Of course, nothing is the same.

To say that we are "held together by
metal and wires" is not an analogy,
not a threat to form a movement that
will change the world, which we hardly
visit anymore, anyway. TV is better,
so are dreams induced by dreams.

These days, we clip the papers and
send each other queries, wondering,
What would Daddy say? Knowing
he would advise sticking with
the workers' union and voting a
straight ticket. Then he would
put on a vaudeville wig and dance

And there's Daddy, dancing away...

You say, *Really? Another century has
already passed?* And I have to tell you
yes, kiddo—it's to laugh, don't you
think? I say you are the only one
who knows me now, why I prefer
to be half Vulcan, to fight my battles
in the ruins of a planet with two suns
and an immortal moon. You are
invited to come kick down the doors
any time that you're in town—in any
town in any universe near me

because the way I'm going to tell
this story, that's how it all started
in the first place: boy and girl, armed
and dangerous, idiots to the end.

VOICES FROM BEYOND

You know, at this juncture, there are a lot of things that
might be helpful. For example, if voices from beyond
would say something to us. Anything. Even a whisper
at 3 a.m. would be appreciated. Scary, but informative.

True, we have the comfort of the television schedule—
much expanded since our younger days! And we have
certain clues that seem important, such as which buses
run all night and how time exists (if it really does, if
it isn't kidding) inside those little glowing clocks that
keep us company in the dark. We also have the records

of how many shirt pieces the factories once required
from the babushkas, and now, how many buckets the city
wants us to carry back and forth between the gene pool
and the dance of death. Not that any of this is necessarily
unreasonable, given the era and the rules that have been
voted in; it's just that, overall, the rationale seems
to be...well, unsupportable. At least, we suspect that
it is becoming unsupportable. And it is our impression
that others are beginning to feel the same way, too.

So perhaps the plan that we came up with the time
that we were really high is something we should revisit.
All we need is one of those cars with blue headlights
that can get us to the Western Lands, where the sky
is waiting to receive us: night, stars, mysterious occurrences
all lit up under the loving hello of the vapor trails.
Think of the incandescence! Blink once for yes and twice
for more. Proud to be traveling with you again, brothers
and sisters, towards the ark of hope that we almost forgot
we had once gathered together to build with our own hands.

ABRACADABRA

I have been in the woods
asleep under the winding wind.
That was in the last century,
which had the taste of apples in its little breezes
but came to be riddled with technology.
Thus, its years went on and on until they stopped.

And this is also true:
someone reached out her arms to me in "the long ago,"
which I remember: it had a sound running through it—
something like jazz in the afternoon.
And art was stacked in all the corridors:
little boxes of feathers and ballerinas.
Little jewels, little gems that fell from the trees
Oh, the heart breaks. It always does.

when someone reaches out from the long ago.
Goodbye, goodbye then, all you darlings.
Some days the sun breaks into golden rings
that chain us to the sky. But the moon breaks, too,
into the cold, clear slices of the future
that are always served up in the aftermath.
So yes, that is what this must be: the other life,
the one you will wake up to from now on.

No, it is not written, but someone always knows
Thus, abracadabra: is it really a surprise
that it turned out to be you?

BEAUTIFUL DENIZENS OF THE DEEP, DARK NIGHT

When we were alive and well in the long ago,
beautiful denizens of the deep, dark night,
love was in charge. Love ran the power stations,
dealt the drugs, bought the incense from Delhi,
which it paid for in turquoise coins.
It ate chocolate at midnight;
its footprints started fires.

And love named comets in the morning,
sailed down the River of Paradise
in the afternoon. Love promoted a belief
in fortune tellers and ballerinas.
It lived on waterlily soup and white lies.

Which is how girls meet, twirling in the street
with blazing haircuts. With jobs to go to
and insurance to sell. Dressed in iron skirts
and disguised in kitten heels, we typed the
capitalist manifestos while the clerks
were crying in the closet. We couldn't
cry yet. We were still too young.

But worry crept in. Would the imposters
be driven from the recital halls so we
could learn to play guitars? Would the
war end, would peace begin, would
justice ever be served? That's how we
occupied the long middle years, with love

still claiming to be the cause and effect.
But even when it paid the rent
I grew suspicious. It wouldn't drink
coffee with us anymore and always
pretended to have forgotten
to buy cigarettes.

But what I learned in secretary school
is that everyone gets tired.
Everything slows down.
Women take old poets in their arms
and try to pirouette, while in the
busy city of our dreams
women foretell love's resurrection.
They turn on the lights and wait.

So last night,
when I woke up in your arms and said,
Call me Elishka, you thought that I was someone else.
But you and I have married in every impossible decade
that howled outside our door. Love comes and goes
like a ballerina, that's what I say.
Kiss me again and I'll show you how.

ABSENT OF

This is what's left: a purple couch,
a sleeping dog. A meal to be eaten
under a flaring sun, dying in red wrapping.
And this particular piece of writing
being written in absentia.

Absent of: well, let me see—
absent of you, certainly.
Absent of you. Of us, really,
pretty girls in boots and bangles,
burning incense in rented room.
Absent of certain days and nights,
but also their corrosion. And of what
went with you when you fled the fire,

such as the memory of a movie set
where we lived when we thought life was
a movie. The sound of a harpsichord,
which we built when we were the women
who worked for a workman's salary.
Who ate marzipan for lunch. More dogs,
friendly and playful. Beautiful men,
fresh spring days, music in the park.

And now, give me a moment
to turn on the radio. It used to
broadcast messages which,
absent of any more interruptions
(yes love, in thy languid hours),
are just beginning to come through.

A Myth Sitting by a River

When the body and soul separate
in the time of their living years,
which does happen: illness, heartbreak,
unfathomable yearnings—who could
possibly specify the cause? You know it,
you feel it, usually before dawn.
Sometimes, it seems, the soul is so
loosely attached that it can be unmoored
as quickly as a sail being ripped from
its mast by a gust of springtime wind.

Afterwards, the body remains at home
tending to the housekeeping. It sweeps
and sweeps while the soul sits on a
riverbank somewhere, looking at clouds.
The soul, it seems, has kept the best
memories: a silver dress that
knew how to dance, a kiss from mama,
and the one good year. Or maybe two.

What happens next, do you think?
Will these companions ever
meet again? There are great
black birds lifting themselves over
the horizon—war birds, death birds,
or perhaps just birds of passage—
and what they signify is
maybe yes, but maybe no.

At home, a bone in a hand
lifts a broom. A myth sitting
by a river sighs, rises, and feels
the wind gathering once more.
It empties its pockets.
It says goodbye to everything,
which signifies that
it will never be seen again,

that the suicide of the eternal
was unseen by its own bones,
which still persist in tending to the house,
still pluck roses from beside the doorstep
and go to sleep in a bouquet.

LEAVING THIS WORLD

Something has changed, I say, speaking into the dust.
You speak of seabirds in endless flight, meaning that
you agree. And there is more evidence in the way
that each day claps with such small hands, dawning
as slowly as an afterthought. Morning is all mist,
lunchtime sews itself shut at the thought of sex
and fortunetelling. The night reveals that the dead
are so long gone their messages can't be trusted anymore.
Suddenly, a flower in a vase turns its poor head.
A vase shatters on a table, the table crashes through
the floor, all catastrophes that could have been predicted
but each a reason to trust the little piece of feeling
inside that makes you believe that you are leaving
this world. Running across a sunny field on an
empty afternoon. Broken, finished. Free.

MANY MEDICATIONS

In such a late year, such a strange time,
I feel like I have swallowed the moon
and it has congealed inside me into
many medications, all of them as cold
as stones. And there is no evidence
that they are doing any good.

Little balms, little remedies:
there was a time when I could make them
out of anything. Witch them up from a
passing fancy, from a ribbon and a ruby,
a season in the rain.

So yes, in a selfish mood
I chained our sister to my ribs
but soon, I will let her go
because like you, I keep
the empty sky in mind when I
travel from here to there,
from room to room, hoping

I can replace what I have taken
and receive some token in return.
Perhaps a year of silence, a day of love.

In such a scenario I believe
that forgotten footsteps will be heard again
and the moon, who says she cares for no one,
will lend a glance to me before she turns away.

SOBRIQUET

We should have known
when there was dust in our coffee cups
and the cafes wouldn't sell us any cigarettes,
that modern life had become just another
mill wheel, a hammer pounding a glass nail.

And so the girl she should have been
rises from the magician's bed and says good-bye.
Walking along the tortured lanes
of this year and that, she well remembers
those metropolitan evenings in the city of God

when our conversations were as important
as money in a velvet pocket and science
paraded its peacocks in the downtown bars
where we drank to the health of physics

and went home to bang out literature
as if it was possible for art to buy its meals
and pay the rent. As if art did not demand
the total attention of its prisoners
who nonetheless, went on believing
that they had been named as honorees.

And so the girl she should have been
decides to perform the unheard-of feat
of living as a stranger. Although this year
and that refuse to comment, preferring
to stay at home smoking cigarettes in bed,

rumors are spreading among the downtrodden
that the girl she is now has finally earned
the sobriquet *at home in the kasbah*
and is often reborn as water and wind,

though that is another story,
the one in which sorrow drowns
in a lily pond and time at last stands still.

About the Author

During a career that now spans over fifty years, Eleanor Lerman has published numerous award-winning collections of poetry, short stories, and novels. One of the youngest people ever to be named a finalist for the National Book Award in Poetry, she also won the inaugural Juniper Prize from the University of Massachusetts Press and the Lenore Marshall Poetry Prize from the American Academy of Poets, among other accolades. In addition, her fiction has been recognized with numerous awards including the John W. Campbell Award for Best Book of Science Fiction and being shortlisted for The Chautauqua Prize. She has also received a Guggenheim Fellowship for poetry as well as fellowships from the National Endowment for the Arts for poetry and the New York Foundation for the Arts for fiction. Her most recent work, *The Game Café: Stories of New York City in Covid Time* (Mayapple Press, December 2022), won the Pinnacle Book Achievement Award and was nominated for the W.S. Porter Prize. *www.eleanorlerman.com*

Recent Titles from Mayapple Press...

Cati Porter, *Small Mammals,* 2023
> Paper, 78pp, $19.94 plus s&h
> ISBN 978-1-952781-15-5

Eleanor Lerman, *The Game Cafe,* 2022
> Paper, 160pp, $22.95 plus s&h
> ISBN 978-1-952781-13-1

Goria Nixon-John, *The Dark Safekeeping,* 2022
> Paper, 92pp, $19.85 plus s&h
> ISBN: 978-1-952781-11-7

Nancy Takacs, *Dearest Water,* 2022
> Paper, 84pp, $19.95 plus s&h
> ISBN: 978-1-952781-09-4

Zilka Joseph, *In Our Beautiful Bones,* 2021
> Paper, 108pp, $19.95 plus s&h
> ISBN: 9780-1-952781-07-0

Ricardo Jesús Mejías Hernández, tr. Don Cellini,
Libro de Percances/Book of Mishaps, 2021
> Paper, 56pp, $18.95 plus s&h
> ISBN: 978-952781-05-6

Eleanor Lerman, *Watkins Glen,* 2021
> Paper, 218pp, $22.95 plus s&h
> ISBN: 978-1-952781-01-8

Betsy Johnson, *when animals are animals,* 2021
> Paper, 58pp, $17.95 plus s&h
> ISBN: 978-1-952781-02-5

Jennifer Anne Moses, *The Man Who Loved His Wife,* 2021
> Paper, 172pp, $20.95 plus s&h
> ISBN: 978-1-936419-96-8

Judith Kunst, *The Way Through,* 2020
> Paper, 76pp, $17.95 plus s&h
> ISBN: 978-1-936419-98-2

Ellen Stone, *What Is in the Blood,* 2020
> Paper, 72pp, $17.95 plus s&h
> ISBN 978-1-936419-95-1

For a complete catalog of Mayapple Press publications, please visit our website at *mayapplepress.com*. Books can be ordered direct from our website with secure on-line payment using PayPal, or by mail (check or money order). Or order through your local bookseller.